W9-CKM-731

Chile

by Cynthia Klingel and Robert B. Noyed

Content Adviser: Delmarie Martinez, Ph.D.,
Department of Spanish Language and Literature,
University of Central Florida

Social Science Adviser: Professor Sherry L. Field,
Department of Curriculum and Instruction, College of Education,
The University of Texas at Austin

Reading Adviser: Dr. Linda D. Labbo,
Department of Reading Education, College of Education,
The University of Georgia

COMPASS POINT BOOKS

Minneapolis, Minnesota

FIRST REPORTS

Compass Point Books
3722 West 50th Street, #115
Minneapolis, MN 55410

Visit Compass Point Books on the Internet at *www.compasspointbooks.com* or e-mail your request to *custserv@compasspointbooks.com*

Cover: Cuernos del Paine in Torres del Paine National Park, Chile

Photographs ©: Tom Till, cover; Unicorn Stock Photos/Andre Jenny, 4, 5, 10, 42–43; Hulton Getty/Archive Photos, 7, 19, 21; Reuters/Luis Chiang/Hulton Getty/Archive Photos, 8; AFP/Corbis, 9; Paul Almasy/Corbis, 11; Reuters/Claudia Daut/Hulton Getty/Archive Photos, 12, 23; Pablo Corral V/Corbis, 13; Trip/M. Barlow, 14, 16, 29; Reuters/Martin Thomas/Hulton Getty/Archive Photos, 15, 28, 32; Francis E. Caldwell/Visuals Unlimited, 17; Macduff Everton/Corbis, 18; Trip/BB Holdings BV, 22; Reuters/Juda Ngwenya/Hulton Getty/Archive Photos, 24; Buddy Mays/Corbis, 25; Erwin C. "Bud" Nielsen/Visuals Unlimited, 26, 38; Hubert Stadler/Corbis, 27; Trip/Eric Smith, 30–31; Trip/C. Hamilton, 33, 34; Trip/R. Belbin, 35; Robert Fried/Tom Stack & Associates, 36; Bonnie Flamer/Photo Network, 39; Barbara Gerlach/Visuals Unlimited, 40; Digital Stock, 41; Chris Barton Photos UK, 45.

Editors: E. Russell Primm, Emily J. Dolbear, and Deb O. Unferth
Photo Researchers: Svetlana Zhurkina and Jo Miller
Photo Selector: Catherine Neitge
Designer: Bradfordesign, Inc.
Cartographer: XNR Productions, Inc.

Library of Congress Cataloging-in-Publication Data
Klingel, Cynthia Fitterer.
   Chile / by Cynthia Klingel and Robert Noyed.
     p. cm. — (First reports)
   Includes bibliographical references and index.
   Summary: An overview of the geography, history, people, and social life and customs of the
South American nation of Chile, the longest country in the world.
   ISBN 0-7565-0183-0 (hardcover)
   1. Chile—Juvenile literature. [1. Chile.] I. Noyed, Robert B. II. Title. III. Series.
   F3058.5 .K55 2002
983—dc21   2001004372

Table of Contents

"¡Hola!" 4

Independence 7

A Mixture of People 10

Made in Chile 13

Arts and Crafts 17

Sports 23

A Variety of Food 27

Holidays 29

The Northern Desert 32

Central Valley 35

The Islands 38

Antarctica and the Pacific Islands 40

Chile Today 42

Glossary 44

Did You Know? 44

At a Glance 45

Important Dates 46

Want to Know More? 47

Index 48

"¡Hola!"

▲ *Children swing in Puerto Natales*

"*¡Hola!* Hello! Welcome to Chile!" You might hear this greeting if you visit Chile. The word *Chile* means "land's end."

Chile is in South America. It is the longest country in the world. Chile is more than 2,650 miles (4,264 kilometers) long.

Chile is south of the **equator**. Its seasons are the opposite of those north of the equator. December is a summer month. June is a winter month.

There are deserts, mountains, and forests in Chile. There are also areas of snow and ice.

Chile is bordered by three countries. Argentina lies

▲ *Hikers climb the icy slopes of Villarica Volcano in Chile's Lake Country.*

along the eastern border. Bolivia is to the northeast.
Peru is to the north. The Pacific Ocean is to the west
and south of Chile.

▲ Map of Chile

Independence

Chile has a long history. More than 20,000 years ago, a tribe of Indians lived in Chile.

In the late 1400s, the Inca Indians came to Chile from Peru. The Inca moved to the Central Valley and lived there for a long time.

In the mid-1500s, Spain attacked the Inca and took their land. The people who lived in Chile did not want Spain to control them. Finally, in 1810, they started a war with Spain.

A man named Bernardo O'Higgins

▲ *Bernardo O'Higgins*

helped the people of Chile fight for independence. People call O'Higgins the Father of Chilean Independence. In 1818, Chile defeated Spain and became free.

Chile has had several wars since then, however. In 1879, Chile fought against Bolivia and Peru. That war

▲ *A parade in 1997 for General Manuel Baquedano, who led Chile to victory in the War of the Pacific and died more than 100 years ago*

is called the War of the Pacific. Chile won the war and claimed more land for itself.

Chile has also had many civil wars. A civil war is a war in which groups of people from the same country fight against each other.

In 1973, army officers led by General Augusto Pinochet took over the government. During his brutal

rule, thousands were arrested and many were killed.

In 1990, an elected president took office. Today, the president chooses other people to help run the government.

◀ *General Augusto Pinochet at a ceremony marking the end of his military command in 1998*

A Mixture of People

▲ Men chat at the cattle market in Temuco.

In Chile, more than 90 percent of the people are mestizos. Mestizos are people who are both Spanish and Native American. Less than 2 percent of Chileans are

European. A small number of Chilean people are Native American.

Spanish is Chile's official language. Many Native Americans speak their own language—Araucanian. Some Chileans speak German or Italian.

Education is very important in Chile. Children must go to elementary school for eight years. In elementary

▲ *Chilean children must go to school for eight years.*

▲ *Chilean students in high school*

school, students study math, Spanish, English, art, science, and writing.

Many children go on to public or private high school for four years. Some students prepare for college. Other students learn job skills. These students need jobs to help support their families.

Made in Chile

▲ *Chile sells many kinds of fruits and vegetables.*

Chile has many strong businesses. Chile sells, or **exports**, a variety of products to other countries. Chile exports ceramics, wood, copper, and iron ore. It also exports fish, fruit, vegetables, and wine.

▲ *A copper mine in Chuquicamata*

People mine copper in Chile. Chile produces more copper than any other country in the world. Iron ore, lead, gold, zinc, silver, and coal are all mined in Chile. People use the coal to make electricity.

Farming is also important in Chile. Most farms are in the Central Valley. Farmers grow grapes that are

▲ A worker unloads a basket of grapes at a Casablanca vineyard.

used to make wine. Chile exports wine to more than fifty countries.

Farmers also grow apples, peaches, pears, corn, wheat, beans, and sugar beets. Many farmers keep cows and chickens, too.

People in northern Chile fish. Coastal fishers catch anchovies, sardines, and mackerel.

▲ A Valparaíso fisherman baits his hooks.

Arts and Crafts

The Chilean people enjoy poetry, music, and dance. They also enjoy theater, painting, and sculpture.

When Europeans moved to Chile, they brought

▲ *A view of Santiago from Cerro Santa Lucia, a park in the center of the city*

▲ *The Municipal Theater, or El Teatro Municipal, in the heart of Santiago*

the arts with them. Now, Chilean art is a mix of European and South American arts. Folk art, or art made by the local people, is also important.

Many Chilean people visit museums and attend theaters in Santiago. Santiago is the largest city and the capital of Chile.

One famous theater in Santiago is the Municipal Theater, or *El Teatro Municipal*. The theater puts on operas, concerts, and ballets with many famous performers.

Some great writers are from Chile. Some Chilean poets are known around the world. Two Chilean poets won the Nobel Prize for literature—Gabriela Mistral in 1945 and Pablo Neruda in 1971. In school, Chilean students learn poetry by heart.

Chilean people enjoy music. They sing and play folk songs at holidays and celebrations.

▲ *Pablo Neruda won the Nobel Prize for literature in 1971.*

Long ago, European **immigrants** brought musical instruments such as guitars with them to Chile. Soon, Chilean people began to play guitars along with their own traditional instruments.

Chilean people love to dance, too. The national dance of Chile is called the *cueca*.

In this dance, musicians play the guitar and the harp while a man and a woman dance together. They are wearing colorful clothes. The man waves his handkerchief and shows off. The woman pretends to be shy. The two dance faster and faster while the audience claps and shouts. People like to dance the cueca at most celebrations.

In Chile, many men and women make beautiful things to look at and to wear. Some people make silver jewelry.

Chileans also make jewelry with bright blue stones called lapis lazuli. Chile is one of only two countries in the world that mine lapis lazuli.

▲ A man and woman dance the cueca, Chile's national dance, in a 1951 performance.

▲ *A Native American woman weaves in Pucon.*

Craftspeople spin wool from the hair of llamas and sheep. They make clothing and blankets.

Chilean people also make beautiful baskets. Chilean farmers and fishers use them in their work. Families use them at home.

Sports

▲ *A Chilean soccer player, left, fights for the ball during a qualifying match for the 2002 World Cup.*

The most popular sport in Chile is soccer, which is called *fútbol*. Soccer is also the national sport. Chilean soccer teams play around the world.

▲ A Chilean rider jumps with his horse during the Olympic Games in Sydney, Australia.

Horse racing is also a favorite sport. In Chile, people raise strong horses. Chileans are proud of their horses.

Many Chileans enjoy fishing and hunting, too. Often, a group of people hunt or fish together.

Skiing is also a favorite sport. In winter, people go to the mountains of Chile to ski.

▲ *A woman skis an unmarked trail in Valle Nevado.*

The rodeo, or *la fiesta huasa*, is also popular. Chilean rodeos are different from rodeos in the United States, though.

In a Chilean rodeo, cowboys do not ride wild horses and bulls that try to buck them off. Instead, cowboys ride trained horses to show their riding skills. The cowboys try to make the horse follow their instructions in the rodeo ring.

▲ *Rodeos are popular in Chile.*

A Variety of Food

▲ *Empanadas on sale in Santiago*

Different kinds of food are popular in different parts of Chile. In some towns, you can find German food because German immigrants live there. They make German pastries and sausages.

Chilean people also eat *empanadas*. They are turnovers usually filled with meat and spices.

Chilean children enjoy eating *sopaipillas* as a treat. Sopaipillas are deep-fried pieces of dough sprinkled with sugar.

A popular drink in Chile is *chicha*. It is made from grapes. At meals and celebrations, Chileans also drink wine. Chile produces many fine wines.

▲ *A worker picks grapes at a vineyard west of Santiago.*

Holidays

▲ *Chilean boys practice for a parade.*

Chile has few national holidays. One of the most important holidays is Independence Day—September 18. On this day, there are festivals and grand parades. People eat empanadas and drink wine and chicha.

▲ Chilean cowboys take part in a festival.

They dance and do the cueca. Independence Day often ends with a Chilean rodeo.

Most holidays in Chile are religious celebrations. On the Sunday after Easter, Chileans celebrate *Domingo de Cuasimodo*. They decorate the town and have a festival in the streets.

Families dress in costumes and ride horses, bicycles, and motorcycles. They parade through their village. Then the *huaso*, or Chilean cowboy, shows his riding skills. He wears the traditional huaso clothing.

The Northern Desert

▲ *A space rover robot takes a test run in the Atacama Desert.*

The northern part of Chile is the driest desert in the world. It is called the Atacama Desert. In most of this desert, it never rains.

In the Atacama Desert, people live in towns by the sea. It is hard to grow food here because it is so dry. The people eat a lot of fish.

People mine here, too. Many minerals are found under the ground.

Part of the Atacama Desert is known as the Valley of the Moon. It is so dry in the Valley of the Moon that nothing can live there.

▲ *The Valley of the Moon*

Geysers are plentiful in the mountains of the desert. A geyser is a place where steam and hot water erupt out of deep holes in the ground. These geysers erupt every morning.

In the southern part of the desert, it rains more than in the northern part. As a result, farmers can grow some crops. People fish here, too.

▲ *These geysers erupt every morning.*

Central Valley

▲ *Fishing boats dock in the harbor of Valparaíso, one of Chile's largest cities.*

The middle part of Chile is called the Central Valley. It is very different from the desert. Rain falls more often, and rivers flow down the mountains.

In the Central Valley, farmers grow vegetables,

▲ A waterfall spills into Todos los Santos Lake in Chile's Lake Country.

fruit, and other crops. They grow grapes to make wine here.

Most Chileans, including the Chilean cowboys, live in the Central Valley. The nation's four largest cities are in the Central Valley. They are Santiago, Valparaíso, Viña del Mar, and Concepción. Almost 80 percent of Chile's people live in these four cities.

South of the Central Valley is an area called the Lake Country. This area has many lakes, mountains, volcanoes, and waterfalls. Visitors come to see its beautiful forests and farms. Tourists like to hike, ski, raft, and climb the mountains.

The Islands

▲ *The Horns of Paine in southern Chile*

South of the Central Valley, Chile breaks up into thousands of islands. A group of many islands is called an **archipelago**. These islands have mountains, **glaciers**, and rushing rivers.

It can be very cold on the islands, and wild storms are common. Many of the islands and mountains are covered in ice and snow. An island in the archipelago called Tierra del Fuego has land that is good for raising sheep.

Few Chileans live in the archipelago. The mountains are steep, and there are few roads. It is necessary to travel by boat.

▲ *A boat glides through the Beagle Channel in Tierra del Fuego.*

Antarctica and the Pacific Islands

▲ *A Chilean research station in Antarctica*

One part of Chile lies in Antarctica. It stretches all the way to the South Pole. This land is covered with ice all year round. Scientists from around the world do research here.

Chile also owns several islands in the South Pacific Ocean. One of these islands is called Easter Island. It is famous for its huge stone carvings called Moai. The other Chilean islands in the South Pacific are called the Juan Fernández Islands.

▲ *Huge statues stand on Easter Island.*

Chile Today

▲ *Children play in a fishing boat at Puerto Natales.*

Chile is a beautiful country with many good businesses. It exports many foods and minerals to

people around the world. The country's government is working to improve life for its people.

Today about 15 million people live in Chile. Whether they live in the mountains, the valleys, the desert, or the cities, Chileans look forward to the future.

If you visit Chile, you will learn more about this special country in South America. When you leave, you may say, "¡Adiós! Good-bye! I enjoyed my visit to Chile!"

Glossary

archipelago—a group of small islands

equator—an imaginary line around the middle of the earth

export—to sell goods to another country

geysers—holes in the ground through which hot water and steam erupt

glaciers—large bodies of ice in very cold areas or on high mountains

immigrants—people who come to settle in another country

Did You Know?

- A tribe of Indians lived in Chile more than 20,000 years ago. Scientists have found mummies and fossils that are more than 10,000 years old.

- Chile is the longest country (north to south) in the world.

- Many of the plants and animals in Chile are found nowhere else in the world.

- Santiago, the capital of Chile, has a population of more than 4 million people.

At a Glance

Official name: Republic of Chile

Capital: Santiago

Official language: Spanish

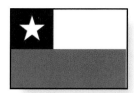

National song: "Cancione Nacionale de Chile"
("National Song of Chile")

Area: 292,257 square miles (756,946 square kilometers)

Highest point: Ojos del Salado, 22,572 feet (6,885 meters)

Lowest point: Pacific Ocean, at sea level

Population: 15,155,495 (2000 estimate)

Head of government: President

Money: Peso

Important Dates

1400s	The Inca come from Peru to Chile.
1500s	Spain takes over Chile.
1810	Civil war in Chile begins.
1818	Chile wins independence from Spain.
1833	A new constitution creates a strong central government.
1879	The War of the Pacific begins.
1883	Chile wins the War of the Pacific.
1925	A new constitution allows Chileans to elect their president.
1973	Army officers led by General Augusto Pinochet take over the government.
1980	Another constitution allows the slow return of democracy.
1990	An elected president named Patricio Aylwin takes office.
2000	Chile has strong economic growth.

Want to Know More?

At the Library

Jacobsen, Karen. *Chile*. Chicago: Childrens Press, 1991.

Pickering, Marianne. *Chile: Where the Land Ends*. New York: Benchmark Books, 1997.

Roraff, Susan. *Chile*. Milwaukee, Wis.: Gareth Stevens Publishing, 1998.

On the Web

Factmonster Almanac

http://www.factmonster.com/ipka/A0107407.html

For more information about the geography and history of Chile

The World Factbook

http://www.cia.gov/cia/publications/factbook/geos/ci.html

For maps, statistics, and other information about Chile

Through the Mail

Chilean Embassy

1732 Massachusetts Avenue, N.W.

Washington, DC 20036

To learn more about Chilean culture and history

On the Road

El Museo del Barrio

1230 Fifth Avenue at 104th Street

New York, NY 10029

212/831-7272

To see exhibits featuring historical and contemporary Latin American art

Antarctica, 40–41
art, 17–18, 20, 22
Atacama Desert, 32–34
Central Valley, 7, 14, 35, 37
clothing, 31
dance, 20, 31
Easter Island, 41
education, 11–12
exports, 13
farming, 14, 16, 22, 34, 35, 37, 39
fishing, 16, 22, 25, 34
folk art, 18, 20, 22
foods, 27–28, 29, 32
government, 9
holidays, 29, 31
horse racing, 25
Inca Indians, 7
Independence Day, 29, 31
islands, 38–39, 41
Juan Fernández Islands, 41
Lake Country, 37
language, 4, 11, 43
literature, 19

mestizos, 10
mining, 14, 20, 33
Mistral, Gabriela, 19
Moai carvings, 41
Municipal Theater, 18–19
music, 19–20
Native Americans, 7, 11
Neruda, Pablo, 19
O'Higgins, Bernardo, 7–8
Pinochet, Augusto, 9
presidents, 9
religion, 31
rodeos, 26
Santiago, 18, 37
skiing, 25, 37
soccer, 23
Spain, 7, 8
sports, 23, 25–26, 37
Tierra del Fuego, 39
tourism, 37
Valley of the Moon, 33
War of the Pacific, 9
weather, 5, 32, 35, 39

About the Authors

Cynthia Klingel has worked as a high school English teacher and an elementary school teacher. She is currently the curriculum director for a Minnesota school district. Cynthia Klingel lives with her family in Mankato, Minnesota.

Robert B. Noyed started his career as a newspaper reporter. Since then, he has worked in school communications and public relations at the state and national level. Robert B. Noyed lives with his family in Brooklyn Center, Minnesota.